Introdi

Situated amid rolling countrysid
and many of the surrounding hills
Bronze Age and the Roman period. The
Saint Mary and is late medieval, although _____ a religious foundation
here since the 7th century.

The surrounding hills and woodland have a plethora of footpaths and tracks that are open to the walking public. This book gives walks for various abilities using a combination of these paths. Although most of the walks use Meifod as a starting point, the villages Pont Llogel, Pontrobert, and Bwlch-y-cibau in and adjacent to the Vyrnwy Valley are also included. There is even a short walk around Meifod village showing a brief history of the principal buildings.

Meifod is on the A495 approximately six miles north-west of Welshpool. In the village there is a general store and post office, a bric-a-bac shop, a garage, a garage with hire coaches and a car park with public conveniences.

A detailed description and a map enable each walk to be followed without difficulty. However, please remember that changes may occur at any time. The area contains much woodland and during tree-felling precautionary diversions may be provided from time-to-time. The location of each walk is shown on the back cover and a summary of their key features is also given.

By using a combination of these walks it is possible to walk from Pont Llogel in the west of the valley, through the villages, Dolanog, Pontrobert, Meifod, and continue to Bwlch-y-cibau in the east. The return walk can use a different route.

It is recommended that you use walking boots and, as the weather can be very changeable, appropriate clothing is carried or worn for protection against the elements. The condition of the paths can change with the weather and the season. Some paths can have very muddy patches. If any problems are encountered please telephone Powys County Council on 01597 827688.

Although my name is on the cover as the writer of this publication many people have been involved in its production. I must thank, in particular, Ruth Beardsell, for her help in the compilation of most of these walks. With her husband, Tony, and Vira Price she has led a small team who, together with Powys County Council and the Forestry Commission Wales, have been responsible for way-marking the routes and establishing the stiles. I must also thank Norman and Carole Jones who have accompanied me on the majority of the walks.

Please observe The Countryside Code, and enjoy your walking.

WALK I

PONT LLOGEL TO DOLANOG

DESCRIPTION This is a walk along lanes, tracks and footpaths of approximately four hours duration. It is suitable for the moderately fit and sure-footed, sensible shoes are a must. Starting from the car-park in Pont Llogel the outward journey along the River Vyrnwy for about 500 metres and then follows Glyndŵr's Way before turning south over the hills to Dolanog. There are excellent views of the rolling countryside. The return walk is along the north-east bank of the River Vyrnwy. The walk also uses part of the Ann Griffiths' Way. The length of the walk is about 7½ miles.

Glyndŵr's Way is a 135 mile trail in the heart of Wales dedicated to Owain Glyndŵr who was the last native Welsh person to hold the title Prince of Wales. He was a descendant of the Princes of Powys. On September 16, 1400, Glyndŵr instigated the Welsh Revolt against the rule of Henry IV of England. Although initially successful, the uprising was eventually put down. Glyndŵr was last seen in 1412 and was never captured, nor tempted by Royal Pardons and never betrayed. His final years are a mystery. The trail begins in Knighton and meanders through the moorland, farmland and woodland of mid-Wales to finish in Welshpool.

The Ann Griffiths Walk is a 7 mile course meandering down the Vyrnwy Valley from Pont Llogel to Pontrobert and is named after the famous Ann Griffiths. She was a Welsh poet and writer of Methodist hymns. She was born as Ann Thomas in 1776 to a tenant farmer from village of Llanfihangel-yng-Ngwynfa and was brought up in the Anglican Church, but joined the Methodist movement after hearing the preaching of Rev. Benjamin Jones of Pwllheli, in 1796. Following the deaths of both her parents, she married Thomas Griffiths, a farmer from the parish of Meifod and an elder of the Methodist church. She died following childbirth aged 29.

START The forestry car park, at Pont Llogel. Grid Ref: SJ 032157

DIRECTIONS Pont Llogel is on the B4395 between Llangadfan and Llanfyllin. From Welshpool take the A458 towards Dollgellau. After Llangadfan turn right onto the B4395. Pont Llogel is about 4 miles from Llangadfan. The car park is situated on the right, just over the bridge on a bend.

1 At the start of the walk there are information boards about Owain Glyndŵr and the area. From here take the gravelled track out of the car park following the river. After about a kilometre go over the stile into a pasture and continue following the river and cross a wooden bridge with a wooden gate at each end.

2 Bear left and continue straight up this field keeping the boundary to your right. On reaching the end of this field, pass through a gate and continue in the same direction, but now the field boundary is on your left. Cross over two stiles, the second one is by a gate and leads into a lane. Cross the lane and take the farm track opposite. At the farm pass to the right of the house and turn right behind the buildings. Go over the stile by the gate and continue up a green lane below woodland on your left. Go through the gate and continue along the green lane, passing through three gates. After the third gate turn right to skirt around the farm. Go through a gate and into the lane.

3 Turn right along the lane which drops down to a stream and then climbs up again. At the top turn left onto a track which continues uphill. After going over a stile by a gate the ground levels out. Pause for a while and admire the extensive views behind you. Continue along the green lane which is damp in places and becomes wider as you follow it further. After about half a kilometre from the last stile, go over another stile by a gate. Continue along the track for about another half a kilometre and then go over a stile by a gate on your right. This is marked with a yellow footpath disc and an acorn.

4 Here you will leave Glyndŵr's Way. Go through fields *from where there are extensive views*. At the third stile turn right

2

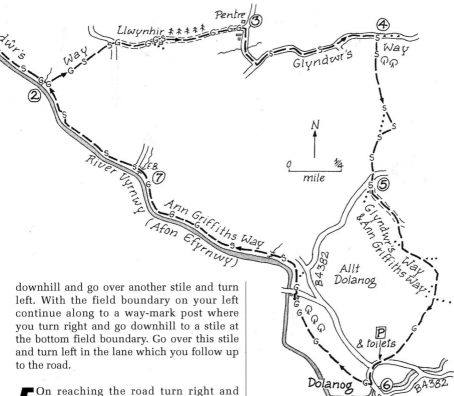

downhill and go over another stile and turn left. With the field boundary on your left continue along to a way-mark post where you turn right and go downhill to a stile at the bottom field boundary. Go over this stile and turn left in the lane which you follow up to the road.

5 On reaching the road turn right and almost immediately left again over a stile by a metal gate. This is marked 'Glyndŵr's Way and Ann Griffiths' Way'. Follow the eight way-marked and finger posts over the moorland admiring the views as you go. The path then goes very steeply downhill and eventually joins a track at a ninth way-marked post. Turn right and follow this track through a metal gate and into the village of Dolanog.

6 Pass the car park, toilets and chapel and turn left at the road. Go past the church and through the gate on the right into the field. The footpath is marked with a finger post. Cross two fields, in each case to a gate in the far left corner. At the second gate you will enter a farm area. Pass through another gate with the house on your left and the barn on your right. On reaching the lane turn right and after a few metres pass through the gate on the left that is marked with a finger-post. You are now on the Ann Griffiths' Way.

7 Keeping the river on your left continue over two stiles and across a plank bridge. Next go through a wooden gate, then a gate and go into a small wood. After going though another gate go across another plank bridge and over the wooden stile on the left. Go over another stile and pass through another small wood. At the end of this woodland pass over another stile and you will rejoin the gravel track leading to the car park at Pont Llogel.

3

PONTROBERT TO DOLANOG AND BACK

DESCRIPTION This walk is Pontrobert to Dolanog and uses mainly tracks and footpaths. The walk is for the moderately fit, and sensible shoes are recommended. Much of the walk follows the River Vyrnwy. The outward walk is along part of Glyndŵr's Way and follows the south bank of the river and there are places where one can picnic on the river bank. The return is to the north of the river, but much of the walk is high up from the river. This is a 6½ mile walk taking about 3 hours.

START The car park at outside the Post Office at Pontrobert. Grid Ref: SJ 108127

DIRECTIONS From Welshpool, take the A490 northwards. After 7 miles, turn left onto the Meifod road (signposted) and follow it to Meifod. Go through the village and over the bridge with the traffic lights to the 'S' bends. Take the road to the right to Pontrobert. At the end of this road in the village turn left and the car park is over the bridge and on the left. There are picnic tables here.

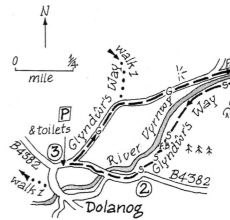

I After leaving the car park at Pontrobert turn left and follow the road. After a short way up the hill take the first road on the right (opposite the Community Centre). Continue for about 300 metres until the road bends sharply to the left. You take the track to the right and go across the cattle grid and pass the red brick houses on your right. At the junction with a track leading to a farm on your right go straight ahead over a cattle grid by a gate. The track will take you over another cattle grid and eventually go downhill towards a house. Just before reaching the house go across the stile on your right into the field and go around the house to return to the track which is now much rougher. At the end of the track go over the stile and follow the green track through the ferns to the riverside. Go through the wood and emerge into a field with a stone cottage on your left.

Go over two more stiles and then follow the track uphill and over a field. The track then re-enters woodland and goes downhill to a stile by a wooden gate. Go over this stile and the footbridge beyond. Go over another stile into a field which you cross to a stile over which you emerge onto a road.

2 Turn right and follow the road. After the 'Dolanog' sign cross the private bridge on your right and pass uphill between two white cottages. At the top of this road opposite a chapel you turn sharp right. *You can turn left where there are toilets on your left. You can visit the church in the village or take refreshment at the tea shop.*

3 Follow the road which becomes a track, continue going through a gate. When the track forks take the right fork and continue along the main track. Take another right fork along the main track and go through another gate. *Take in the view ahead along the valley.* At the next fork again take the right route and pass a waymark to a footbridge. Just after crossing the bridge take the left fork uphill and go around a field which is on your right.

4 When you reach a fingerpost turn right leading to a gate leading into woodland. At the next waymark take the right fork and continue to another waymark where you again take the right fork. Continue to another waymark where track becomes better surfaced and leads downhill to a road.

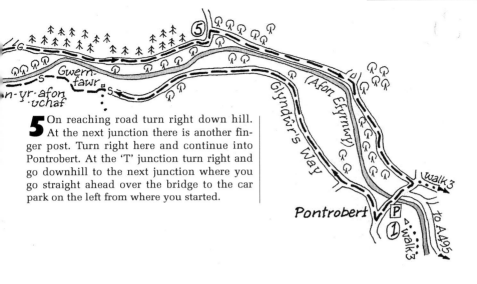

5 On reaching road turn right down hill. At the next junction there is another finger post. Turn right here and continue into Pontrobert. At the 'T' junction turn right and go downhill to the next junction where you go straight ahead over the bridge to the car park on the left from where you started.

Plas Dolanog

PONTROBERT TO DOLOBRAN

DESCRIPTION This walk is Pontrobert to Dolobran and uses mainly tracks and footpaths. The walk is for the moderately fit, and sensible shoes are recommended. The outward walk is along part of Glyndŵr's Way and the return follows the south bank of the River Vyrnwy. This is a 3½ mile walk taking about 2 hours. When in Pontrobert visit The John Hughes Chapel. John Hughes (1755-1854) was a Methodist preacher and writer of hymns who lived and died at Pontrobert. The chapel bearing his name was built in 1800.

START The car park at outside the Post Office at Pontrobert. Grid Ref: SJ 108127

DIRECTIONS From Welshpool, take the A490 northwards. After 7 miles, turn left onto the Meifod road (signposted) and follow it to Meifod. Go through the village and over the bridge with the traffic lights to the 'S' bends. Take the road to the right to Pontrobert. At the end of this road in the village turn left and the car park is over the bridge and on the left. There are picnic tables here.

1 After leaving the car park at Pontrobert turn right and go over the river bridge and turn right again. After about 100 metres turn left uphill. At the crossroads where there is a chapel on your left turn right and follow the lane. Just after the cottage Bryn-y-fedwen the lane becomes a track to a gate. *Admire the views.* Go through the gate and the track bears left and continues to another gate through which you turn left. This track is very muddy. Continue until a gate is reached on your left. Go through this gate and turn right. Keep to the edge of the field and at the corner turn left and with the trees on our right pass the waymark and continue to the small gate. Once through this gate go downhill keeping the field boundary on your right until you reach another waymark. Turn right leaving Glyndŵr's Way to continue as a track straight ahead.

2 Turn right through the gate and immediately right through a small gate. Continue straight ahead to the corner of the field. *The 17th Century Quaker Friends' Meeting House is on your right. This was built by the Lloyd family of Lloyd's Bank fame. The building is hidden to avoid the persecution prevalent at the time.* At the field corner turn left, and with the field boundary on your right go uphill to a stile. *The views on your left are worth tarrying for a while.* Once over the stile continue downhill across the next field to the stile facing you and to the right of the farm. Go over the stile and turn right in the lane. Follow this lane to the 'T' junction with the road and turn left. Go along the road and over the river bridge. At about 250 metres after the bridge turn right onto a track which is a bridleway.

3 Follow the track up through the trees and go through the gate marking the entrance to Old Forge Mill. Go across the yard at the mill and through a gate and a pair of gates onto a hedge-lined green track. Pass a lily pond on your left and go across a wooden bridge and through a gate into the woodland facing you. The river is on your right. There is a ditch on your left which was once the leet to the mill. Go through two more gates at the end of the woodland and continue until you emerge into a yard. Cross the yard with the house on your right and continue through the gate facing you and along the lane until you reach the car park from where you started.

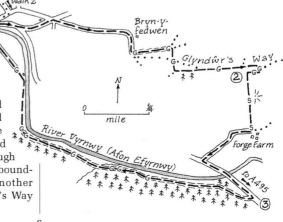

WALK 4

FFRIDD MATHRAFAL

DESCRIPTION This is a walk of moderate ability along forestry tracks and footpaths. There are a few muddy footpaths so sensible shoes are a must. The walk is about 4 miles in length and should be about 2 hours should be allowed. There are waymarks throughout in the form of poles with coloured bands.

START The entrance to Ffridd Mathrafal. Grid Ref: SJ 112100

DIRECTIONS Mathrafal Forest is on the A495 Oswestry to Neuadd Bridge road, where it joints the A458 Welshpool to Dollgelau road. The entrance is situated about three miles west of Meifod. From Welshpool, take the A490 northwards. After 3 miles, turn left onto the Meifod road (signposted) and follow it through Meifod. Pass over the bridge with traffic lights and continue on the A495, the entrance is on the right about one after the bends and junction with the road to Pontrobert. Alternatively, from the west, turn of the A458 onto the A495 and the entrance is on the left shortly after the Tan House Inn.

I Pass through the gate at the entrance and continue uphill along the forestry track. On meeting the junction of the tracks, with the caravan site on your right, take the track to the left, between trees marked with a green 'C'. This track eventually narrows to a path. Pass three waymarks with red, blue and green bands and go uphill through the forest. On reaching a square post on your left there is a junction of paths. Take the left path uphill. The path is very muddy. Pass the gate a gate on your left and continue five waymarks with red and blue bands until you reach a small clearing with a picnic table.

2 Here you come to a 'T' junction with another path. Turn left past the square post on your right, pass a waymark with a single red band and later another square post and single red-banded waymark. When the path joins the forestry track turn left and continue for about 300 metres *to take in the views of Dolobran and Pontrobert.*

3 Retrace your steps along the forestry track, but continue downhill until you see a narrow green path going downhill on your left. Go down this path passing the waymark with a single red band on your right. Continue through the oak trees and woodland passing another waymark to a wooden handrail. Here there is another 'T' junction with a track. Turn right here and continue passing the red waymark until you meet the forestry tracks were there are picnic tables and a pool on your right.

4 Turn right here and follow the track downhill – *the hill facing you is Bryn y Saethau (Bridge of Arrows, an ancient settlement)* – until you meet the track which you came up earlier. The caravan site is on your left. Turn left here and continue downhill and through the gate at the entrance.

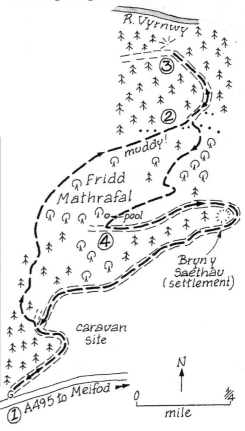

7

WALK 5

MEIFOD TO COED-COWRHYD, DOLOBRAN & HEALING WELL

DESCRIPTION This is an 8 mile walk along lanes, tracks and footpaths of approximately 4½ hours duration. It is suitable for the moderately fit and sure-footed, sensible shoes are a must. This is a longer route for the energetic walker. For a shorter route one can return along the west river bank (**WALK 9**). Starting from Meifod the outward route takes you below Gallt yr Ancr (**WALK 11**) and follows Glyndŵr's Way to Dolobran and then returns along the banks of the River Vyrnwy. The route then goes through Newbridge (**WALK 8**) to the Healing Well, Ffynnon y Clawdd Llesg, in Spout Wood. Many local parishes have their medicinal wells which were the focus of ancient customs. Sadly, these customs had ceased by the mid-19th century and many of the wells became neglected. Ffynnon y Clawdd Llesg, set high in the hills in a remote corner of Meifod parish, has had its fair share of neglect but has never been entirely forgotten. The mineral water is supposed to cure 'wounds, sprains and scrofulous disorders'. The water is not for drinking, but for bathing in. Last century the spring had a timber bathing house built around it. This has now gone, but the cistern and some of the flooring can still be seen. The woodwork was 'cut and scored with the names of those who had benefited from the waters'. An inscription above the spout read, 'Every wound to be held for twenty minutes under the spout three times a day' (*quotations from Vol. 9 of Montgomeryshire Collections and 'The Holy Wells of Wales', Francis Jones*).

START The car park, at Meifod. Grid Ref: SJ 153132

DIRECTIONS From Welshpool, take the A490 northwards. After 7 miles, turn left onto the Meifod road (signposted) and follow it to Meifod. In the village turn right at the junction where on your right there is a car park and toilets.

1 Turn right out of the car park, and take the second left turn (after the black and white house on the left). Follow this lane until a bend in the road. Go through the gate on the left and continue up the path on Glyndŵr's Way until another gate is reached. After this gate keep the field boundary on your right until you come to a stile leading to the road.

2 Turn right and continue until you see a stile on your right. Go over this stile and diagonally across the field and over another stile onto the lane again. Turn right and continue around the bend and uphill, but ignore Glyndŵr's Way where it turns left towards the farm of Coed-Cowrhyd. Continue straight ahead passing through two gates. Keep the fence on your right and pass through another gate. Keep the fence on your left through fields. The path bends to the left until a ford is reached at the bottom.

3 Go through the gate on your left, cross the ford, walk straight on with the pool on your right and go over the stile into a large field. Walk the length of this field with the hedge on your left. On reaching the track turn left, go up the rise and turn left through the gate where the ground is muddy. Cross the field diagonally to the right. Go over the stile in the corner at the end of the trees, go down behind the Quaker Meeting House. *The Quaker Meeting House was built in the 17th Century by the Lloyd family who were famous for founding Lloyd's Bank.* Turn right through the gate.

4 Turn right again, go through the wicket gate and pass in front of the Chapel. At the field boundary turn left, and follow the edge of the field through this field, go over the stile and into the next field. Continue across the field and go over the stile into the lane and turn right. Go down the lane and around the corner in front of the bungalow and turn left over the stile and continue straight ahead. The path takes you up a slight rise and then over a stile into a field.

Turn right and cross this field to a stile, go over the stile and through the gate and then go through the gate on the right and along the left hand side of the next field by a ditch.

5 Near the river end of this field go over the bridge and through a gate and then turn immediately right. The path is then way-marked all the way,

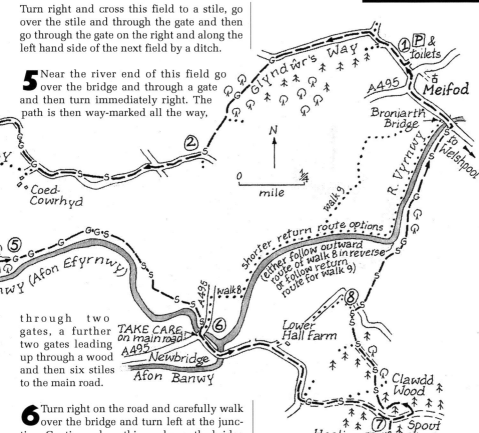

through two gates, a further two gates leading up through a wood and then six stiles to the main road.

6 Turn right on the road and carefully walk over the bridge and turn left at the junction. Continue along this road over the bridge and then straight ahead and uphill at the junction at Lower Hall Farm. At the top of the hill the road turns right and then shortly you turn left onto the forestry track opposite a half-timbered house. Go through the gate and then over a stile by a gate, where you continue straight ahead along the forestry track.

7 On the right there is a narrow path leading off to the right which leads uphill to the Healing Well. After visiting the Well retrace your steps to the forestry track and turn right. Continue until you turn left onto a narrow overgrown path by a waymark. Go down this path through Clawdd Wood and over a stile into a field which you cross with the boundary on your right. Go over a stile by a gate onto a track and turn right

over another stile into a field. Keep the field boundary on your right and continue down and over a stile by a gate. Cross the field and over another stile by a gate into a road.

8 Turn right and then around the corner, go left over a stile by a gate. Again keep the field boundary on your right and go through the gap and across the next field. Go over the stile and cross the next field to a rough track leading to a stile and wooden bridge by the River Vyrnwy. With the river on your left, go through two gates and a stile and then eventually over a stile into the road. Turn left and go over the bridge to the 'T' junction, turn right on the main-road and then first left. The car park where you started is on your right.

FOEL, SPOUT & CLAWDD WOODS

DESCRIPTION This circular strenuous walk of 7½ miles takes you through three woods. The first of these woods is Foel, meaning 'Bare Hill'. Second, you will come to Spout Wood where there is a healing well (**WALK 5**) which is reputedly associated with the old saints of Meifod. Finally, you will come to Clawdd Wood, named after the earthwork, 'Clawdd Llesg' which was built to defend the Vale of Meifod and the Guilsfield Valley. Almost all the trees are now recently planted conifers, but the land has always been wooded. The ancient native woodland was progressively destroyed from the 1920s to the 1950s until the replanting was undertaken by the Forestry Commission. The walk is through fields, along lanes and footpaths. Sensible footwear is a must for this walk, several muddy patches will be encountered. Allow 3½ hours for the walk.

START The car park, at Meifod. Grid Ref: SJ 153132

DIRECTIONS From Welshpool, take the A490 northwards. After 7 miles, turn left onto the Meifod road (signposted) and follow it to Meifod. In the village turn right at the junction where on your right there is a car park and toilets.

I Turn left out of Meifod Car Park and proceed the 50 metres to the main road. Turn right and walk about 100 metres then turn left onto the Guilsfield Road and continue past the bowling green and tennis courts on the left before crossing the River by Broniarth Bridge. Immediately after the bridge go right over the stile and follow the signs along the river bank. After about 300 metres go over a stile into the next field, follow the river bank through two gates and over a stile until the River Vyrnwy bends to the right. After about another 50 metres pass the waymark and go up the track into the field. Cross the field diagonally and then go over a stile. Cross two more fields and then go over a stile into a lane.

2 Turn right and go around the bend in the lane. Go over the stile on the left by a gate. Cross the field and go over another stile by a gate. Continue upwards with the hedge on your left to another stile which leads you into a wood. Follow the track up to the left and over another stile by a gate. Go across the next field above the trees to the left to a stile in the top corner. Once over this stile go into the forestry and follow the cleared path around and up to the forestry track. Here you can make a detour to the right to the Healing Well. This is done by following the track for about 100 metres and then left up the way-marked path to the well (**WALK 5**). After seeing the well, retrace your steps to the way-marked path which will now be on your right. If you do not go to the well turn right for a few metres along the forestry track and go along the way-marked path on your left. Continue with the trees on your left and through the gate at the top. Cross the field, go through the trees, over two stiles and onto a track above a house and buildings. Turn left and go through two gates and enter the area of the buildings to the finger post on your left. Walk down through an avenue of trees and go over another stile into a field. Cross this field and then after about 200 metres enter the woods on your left by another stile.

3 Follow this path for about half a mile along the inner edge of the wood until a stile is reached. Go over this stile into the lane and turn left. Go slightly downhill and after about 400 metres there is a stile hidden in the hedge on the right. Go over this stile into the field. Cross the fields by going over three more stiles until another stile is reached leading you into another lane. Cross this lane and go over another stile marked 'Glyndŵr's Way'. Go around the field with the wood on your right until you reach a way-marked post. Here you turn left and go down into the valley. Go over the stile, cross another field, go over another stile and then continue uphill on the other side of the valley to a stile opposite a white house. Go over the stile into the lane and turn left leaving Glyndŵr's Way.

4 After about 300 metres the lane turns sharply left. Here you go straight ahead through a gate and follow the way-marks across three fields, crossing two stiles). *This is a place where you can stop a short while to admire the views.* Eventually you will reach a stile which leads to another lane. Turn right and go down the lane. After about 200 metres you will reach a junction with a house on your right and a farm on your left. Turn right and follow this lane to a crossroads. Go straight across and after about 100 metres there is a stile on your right next to a gate leading to a track up to a half timbered house. Go over the stile and follow the track uphill through the wood to another stile on your left. Go over this stile and continue upwards with the fence on your left and then you will find yourself in Cobham's Garden.

5 At the bottom of Cobham's Garden go over the stile into the wood, go down through the wood passing a waymark on your left, then your right and another on your left. Eventually you will reach a stile into a field. Go diagonally left across the field following the track to a stile. Once over this you will be in a lane. Turn right and follow this lane for about 250 metres until it turns sharply right. Here you go over the stile on your left and go straight down the first field with the hedge on your left. Pen-y-lan Hall is on your right. Go over a stile then cut across diagonally to another stile by a gate, cross the next field and then eventually emerge at the stile next to Broniarth Bridge which leads you into the road at the point where you entered the field by the river earlier. Turn left and retrace your steps into Meifod

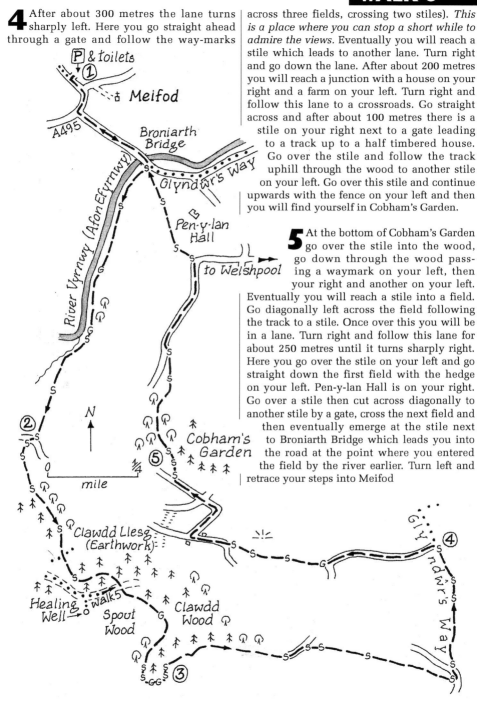

GLYNDŴR'S WAY: MEIFOD TO MAESMAWR

DESCRIPTION This is a walk along lanes, tracks and footpaths of approximately four hours duration. It is a 7½ mile strenuous walk suitable for the fit and sure-footed, sensible shoes are a must. Starting from the car-park in Meifod the outward route takes you along Glyndŵr's Way up the north side of Broniarth Hill. The summit of the hill is about 270 metres above sea level. Although the hill is still wooded much felling has taken place in recent years. Part way along the walk and to the east of Broniarth Hill you will see Llyn Du pool. Near Maesmawr the walk turns west off Glyndŵr's Way through woodland before heading north to Meifod along the east bank of the River Vyrnwy.

START The car park, at Meifod. Grid Ref: SJ 153132

DIRECTIONS From Welshpool, take the A490 northwards. After 7 miles, turn left onto the Meifod road (signposted) and follow it to Meifod. In the village turn right at the junction where on your right there is a car park and toilets.

I On leaving the car park turn left, and continue to the main A495 road. Turn right along the main road and take the first left signposted 'Recreation Facilities'. Continue over the River Vyrnwy on Broniarth Bridge and take the road on the left, named Ffordd Glyndŵr. After about half a kilometre a bridleway forks to the right and climbs through the forest. Take this bridleway until it takes a turn to the right. Go straight ahead here on the narrower track and still climbing. This track in turn takes a sharp turn to the right, but you still go straight ahead on an even narrower track way-marked with an arrow and an acorn. Continue through the clearing and a gate, where the track becomes a little less steep but enters woodland again. Pass a waymark and then to a gate where there is a brick hut on your left. On passing through this gate you will enter a field with a view of Llyn Du Pool to your right. With the field boundary on your right continue straight ahead and then, at the waymark, turn sharp right through a gate and into the road.

2 Turn right in the road and continue to the cross-roads where you go straight ahead past Bryndial Cottage on your left. *Take note of the views on your right.*

3 At the next road junction, where there is a bungalow, bear right and continue down the road to a Footpath sign on the left. Turn sharp left here and then continue down the track going over two stiles, each by a gate. At the second stile the track emerges into a field, but is marked with waymarks. Pass the derelict brick and corrugated sheeted cottage and barn on your left and go over the stile by the gate. Continue with the field boundary on your left, *but pausing to admire the magnificent views. There was once an iron-age fort on the hill behind you.* Go over the next stile, cross a field and then over a stile by a farm on your right. Turn right through a gate into the lane, and then go over the stile immediately on the left. Cross the field, over a stile by a gate, across another field, over another stile by a gate, and across another field to the waymark by the trees. Skirt the field with trees on your left to a stile where you turn left into the lane.

4 Go the short distance to the gravelled road and turn right, with Garden House on your left. Pass the walled garden and extensive farm buildings on your left and then take the right fork climbing gradually up the hill. On emerging from the tree cover *admire the view* and take the right track through a gate and follow this track downhill. Go through another gate where the track becomes a green lane. Once through the next gate go into the lane and turn left. Pass to the right of the house and buildings through two gates and continue uphill. These are marked as a bridleway. Go uphill to another gate and into a field which you cross to the left of a pond and through a gate. *Just after the pond and before the gate, you may make a detour through another gate on the right*

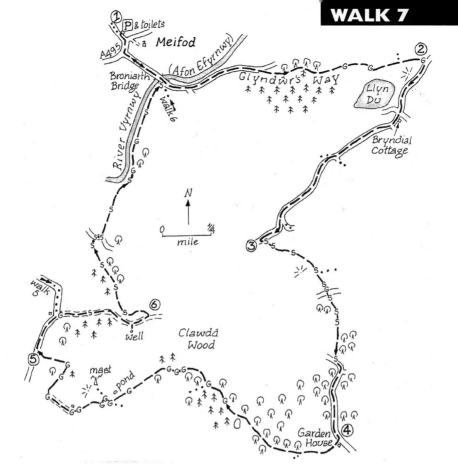

of the field and admire the view from by the mast, and then return to the bridleway. With the field boundary on your right continue for only a few metres until a gate appears on your right. Go through this gate and follow the field down to a gate in front of a house. Pass this house on your right and follow the track through four gates. On emerging over a cattle grid into a road you turn right.

5 Continue along the road and turn right onto the forestry track opposite a half-timbered house. Go through the gate and then over a stile by a gate, where you go straight head along the forestry track and continue until you turn left onto a narrow overgrown path by a waymark.

6 Go down this path through Clawdd Wood and over a stile into a field which you cross with the boundary on your right. Go over a stile by a gate onto the track and turn right over another stile into a field. Keep the field boundary on your right and continue down and over a stile by a gate. Cross the field and over another stile by a gate into a road. Turn right and then around the corner go left over a stile by a gate. Again keep the field boundary on your right and go through the gap and across the next field. Go over the stile and cross the next field to a rough track leading to a stile and wooden bridge by the River Vyrnwy. With the river on your left, go through two gates and then eventually over a stile into the road, which you will recognize as where you went along earlier. Turn left and retrace your steps into Meifod.

NEWBRIDGE

DESCRIPTION This is an easy stroll along the river bank to the tiny hamlet of Newbridge with its small chapel having services once per month. The return is on the opposite side of the river bank. This walk is almost entirely on level ground with a length of about 4 miles, 1½ hours should be allowed. As the walk is across grassland that may be wet, sensible shoes are a must.
START The car park, at Meifod. Grid Ref: SJ 153132
DIRECTIONS From Welshpool, take the A490 northwards. After 7 miles, turn left onto the Meifod road (signposted) and follow it to Meifod. In the village turn right at the junction where on your right there is a car park and toilets.

1 Turn left out of the car park and proceed the 50 metres to the main road. Turn right and cross the road, then walk about 100 metres and turn into the road on the left. Continue past the tennis courts and bowling green on the left. Just before the river and by the wooden building: 'River Level Measurement Centre', go right over two stiles and follow the path along the river bank. Follow the permissive path marked by green way-marks along the edge of the field. After about 200 metres, go over a bridge over a culvert with stiles at either end. Continue for about another 150 metres and go over another stile over an electric fence. After about another 100 metres go over another stile in a hedge. Keep the river on your left and go around the next field (turning right and left around a fence). Go over another stile and straight across the field and over a stile by the poplar trees. Go over another three stiles and the path will eventually bring you to a stile by an old mill house (*Glascoed Mill used to contain a vertical turbine which generated the power when electricity first came to Meifod*) where you will emerge onto a track. Go down this track to the main road noting the remains of several mill wheels on your left.

2 At the main road turn left and walk about 100 metres to the bridge with the traffic lights. TAKE CARE. Cross the bridge and turn left. After about 100 metres you will reach the hamlet of Newbridge with its small chapel. Continue following the lane over another river bridge and turn left at Lower Hall Farm.

3 Continue along the lane until you reach the new bungalow. Go through the gate to the left of the house and follow the path around the left hand edge of the field, through a gate to a stile. Go over the stile back into the lane, turn right and follow the lane around the corner to a stile on your left. Go over this stile, keep the field boundary on your right and go through the gap and across the next field. Go over the stile and cross the next field to a rough track leading to a wooden bridge by the River Vyrnwy. With the river on your left, go through two gates and a stile and then eventually over a stile into the road and turn left.

4 Cross Broniarth Bridge over the river and follow the road to the 'T' junction opposite the telephone kiosk. Turn right here and then take the first turning left. After about 50 metres the car park from where you started will be on the right.

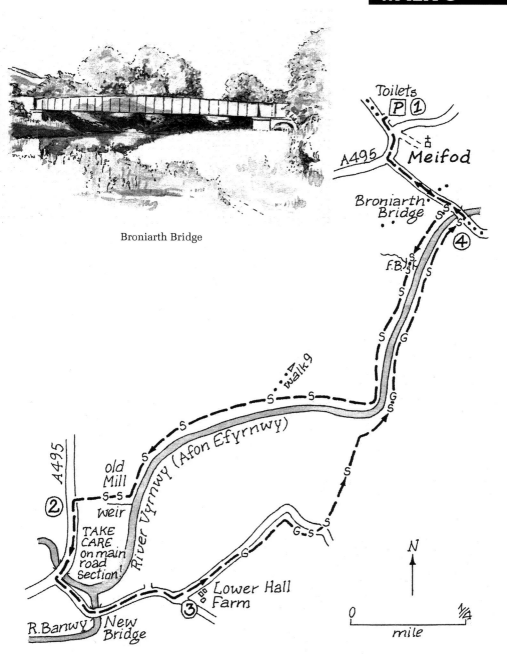

Broniarth Bridge

Toilets
P ① ⛪ **Meifod**
A495

Broniarth Bridge

④

F.B.

River Vyrnwy (Afon Efyrnwy)

walk 9

old Mill
weir
A495
②

TAKE CARE on main road section!

R.Banwy New Bridge

③ Lower Hall Farm

N

0 ¼ mile

WALK 9
BY THE RIVER

DESCRIPTION The River Vyrnwy flows through Meifod on its way from the man-made reservoir of Lake Vyrnwy to the River Severn. It has joined up with the River Banwy at Newbridge, about 1½ miles from Meifod. The water level in the river can vary considerably. Most of the time it is placid with very little flow, but occasionally it is a raging torrent after heavy rains have fallen in the mountains. The flow of water is regulated from the dam at Lake Vyrnwy. This walk is an easy stroll on the level of 2 miles and approximately one hour duration. The walk is mainly through fields and footpaths which can be wet. Sensible shoes are a must.

START The car park, at Meifod. Grid Ref: SJ 153132

DIRECTIONS From Welshpool, take the A490 northwards. After 7 miles, turn left onto the Meifod road (signposted) and follow it to Meifod. In the village turn right at the junction where on your right there is a car park and toilets.

I Turn left out of Meifod Car Park and proceed the 50 metres to the main road. Turn right and walk about 100 metres then turn left and continue past the bowling green and tennis courts on the left. Turn right just after the wooden building: 'River Level Measurement Centre', but immediately before crossing the river and go over the two stiles.

2 Following the river bank using the permissive path marked by green way-marks go along the edge of the field for about 200 metres until a bridge over a culvert is reached. Go over this bridge with stiles at either end and then continue for about another 150 metres to another stile over an electric fence. Go over this stile and after about another 100 metres go over another stile in a hedge. Keep the river on your left and go around the next field (turning right and left around a fence).

3 On reaching a stile by the start of a row of tall poplar trees turn right, but don't go over the stile. Turn right and make for a gate and stile by an oak tree and then diagonally across a field to a stile which appears to be in the middle of nowhere. This stile is used to go over an electric fence when this is in situ. Go through the gate on the left, across the track and over the stile opposite. Follow the way-marks to the dyke.

4 Turn right and go over the stile on the dyke. Walk along the dyke to the road. Go over the stile into the road, turn left and retrace your steps into Meifod.

By the river

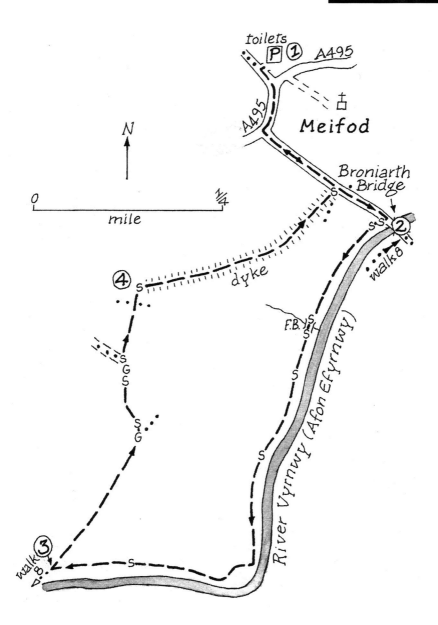

toilets P ① A495
† Meifod
A495
Broniarth
Bridge
walk 8

N

0 ———————— ¼
mile

④ S dyke

F.B. S

River Vyrnwy (Afon Efyrnwy)

G S

S G

③ walk 8 S

ALLT Y MAIN

(ALSO KNOWN AS 'PEAK POINT')

DESCRIPTION This is a strenuous walk of seven miles with a 1000 feet of gradual ascent and a steep route back down. The route on the way up takes the walker through woods of mainly deciduous trees until the forest of fir trees is reached. However, after emerging from the trees, the summit of Allt y Main is bare and grassy. At the summit there is a trigonometry survey point from where there is a 360 degree panoramic view showing the Cambrian Mountains to the west and the Shropshire plain to the east with Meifod down below to the south-west. Notable peaks include Cadair Idris and The Wrekin. The name of the hill when translated into English means 'the narrow hill'. Sensible shoes are recommended. The duration of the walk is about 3½ hours.

START The car park, at Meifod. Grid Ref: SJ 153132

DIRECTIONS From Welshpool, take the A490 northwards. After 7 miles, turn left onto the Meifod road (signposted) and follow it to Meifod. In the village turn right at the junction where on your right there is a car park and toilets.

1 Turn right from Meifod car park and follow the road uphill for about half a mile. Where the road forks take the narrow road marked by a 'No Through Road' sign to the right and continue along the lane and through the gate at the end. Three paths diverge here and each is marked by a colour-coded finger-post.

2 Take the track to the left and marked by the yellow finger post, and then after about 20 metres take the track to the right into the field. Continue up through the field keeping the hedge on your left. On reaching the stile at the top left-hand corner of the field, *tarry awhile and look back to admire the view.* Go over the stile and into the forest and follow the green path through the forest and down onto the forestry track. Turn left onto the track and follow it for the best part of a mile. To your right is a track to a viewpoint overlooking the Glascwm.

3 There is a seat at this viewpoint where you can rest and admire the views. Return to the forestry track and turn right and go around several bends until you see a gravel track going up to the left near a corner in woodland. Ignore this track which is blocked by fallen trees and go around the corner to another track on the left. Go up this track to a 'T' junction of tracks and turn left at the waymark. Follow this track up to the viewpoint. Here there is a seat for you to rest awhile and admire the 360 degree panoramic view. *This is the perfect stop to take refreshment and ponder the views.*

4 Start your descent by retracing your steps through the forest to the forestry track. Turn right and continue until you again come to the track for the Glascwm viewpoint. Turn left, but immediately there is a way-marked track to the right through the forest. Continue down this steep path until you reach another forestry track. Turn right onto the forestry track and then left at the way-marked post around the corner. Turn left again at another way-mark post and continue down the very steep track to the road. Go across the road and left for a few metres and then right and follow the way-marks through the farmyard of 'Bron-y-Maen'. (An alternative route is to take the bridleway left at (**A**) down to the road and then walk CAREFULLY along the road to meet the route at Bron-y-Maen).

5 Continue down the farm lane and right via a gate into the field. Go diagonally across this field and through a metal swinging gate onto the dyke. Turn right and continue along the path which follows the dyke. Pass over a stile, a small wooden bridge and three more stiles when following the track along the dyke. On reaching the road go over the stile and turn right. At the 'T' junction with the telephone kiosk opposite, turn right back to the village. After about 50 metres turn left and the car-park from where you started will appear on your right.

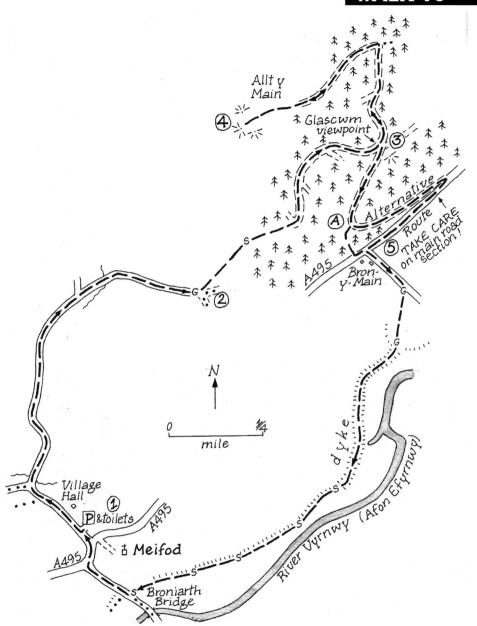

Allt y Main

④

Glascwm viewpoint

③

Alternative Route TAKE CARE on main road section!

Ⓐ

A495

⑤

Bron-y-Main

S

G

②

N

0   ¼
mile

dyke

G

G

S

River Vyrnwy (Afon Efyrnwy)

Village Hall

①

P &toilets

A495

⛪ Meifod

A495

S

S

S

S

S

S

Broniarth Bridge

WALK 11

GALLT YR ANCR – ANCHORITE'S HILL

(ALSO KNOWN AS DYFFRYN HILL)

DESCRIPTION The route on the way up takes the walker through woods of mainly deciduous trees (beeches, oaks and yews) interspersed with some evergreen trees. However, after emerging from the wood, the summit of Gallt yr Ancr is bare and grassy. There is a panoramic view in all directions with Meifod to the east. Nobody quite knows the origin of the name, but presumably a hermit once inhabited this place. This walk is of 2½ miles and about 45 minutes should be allowed. A flight of over 90 steep steps is encountered and one should be fairly fit for this strenuous walk. Sensible shoes are a must.

START The car park, at Meifod. Grid Ref: SJ 153132

DIRECTIONS From Welshpool, take the A490 northwards. After 7 miles, turn left onto the Meifod road (signposted) and follow it to Meifod. In the village turn right at the junction where on your right there is a car park and toilets.

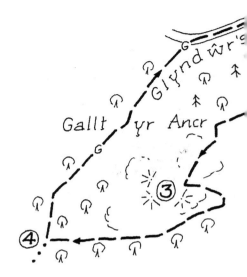

I Turn right out of Meifod Car Park and proceed past the Village Hall for about 100 metres to a short signposted lane on the left just after the road 'Maesyllan' and before the old black and white timbered house. This looks like a driveway but leads to a junction of two footpaths. Take the right path go up a few steps and then over a stile and climb the long steep steps through the woods.

2 At the top of the steps the path takes a left turn along a tree-lined ridge. There are some steep wooded drops on either side, but if you keep to the path there should be no danger. When the path dips a little there is a waymark post where a path comes up from behind on the right. Do not go straight ahead, but take the path that turns left. Go up past a waymark post on the right and then

two waymark posts on the left before arriving at a stile. After going over this stile continue to the summit by going straight ahead on the track through the ferns. Ignore the waymark on the stile pointing to the track to the left. The summit gives you gives you a panoramic view of the area. *This is the perfect stop to take refreshment and ponder the views. The River Vyrnwy can be seen emerging into view in the west winding through the valley to the south and disappearing from view to the east. To the north are the Cheshire plains.*

3 From the summit continue to the lower summit and then into the dip between this and the lower hill ahead. Turn left here, then follow the path which widens around the base of this lower hill.

4 At the fence ahead will be found a way-marked post where you turn right onto Glyndŵr's Way. Continue down this path where you will come to a gate. Go through the gate and continue downwards through the woodland until the gate into the narrow

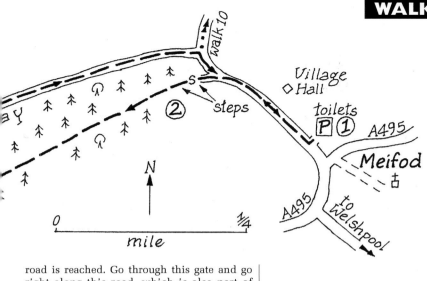

road is reached. Go through this gate and go right along this road, which is also part of Glyndŵr's Way. At the road junction at the end turn right into Meifod.

Dyffryn Hill

RHÔS-Y-GLASCOED FROM MEIFOD

DESCRIPTION The outward walk is across fields and along a woodland track to Alltfawr and Rhôs-y-glascoed. The return follows a track to the north of Gally yr Ancr (**WALK 11**). It is fairly easy covering about 5 miles and taking about 2 hours, but sensible shoes are a must. There are magnificent views.

START The car park, at Meifod. Grid Ref: SJ 153132

DIRECTIONS From Welshpool, take the A490 northwards. After 7 miles, turn left onto the Meifod road (signposted) and follow it to Meifod. In the village turn right at the junction where on your right there is a car park and toilets.

I After leaving the car park and recycle centre at Meifod turn right and follow the road. Go past the white cottages and then take the second turn on the left through a gate and follow the track with the rear of a house on your left. Go along a tree lined path (this can be muddy) and through a gate. Keep the edge of the field on your left and then go through a gate. Cross the field with the black and white house ('The Goetre') on your right. Go straight across the drive to this house to the waymark and then the stile and wooden bridge. Turn right and go through the gate and diagonally right across the field and uphill towards the wood. Go through the gate in the corner of the field and onto the green path and then along the tree lined path keeping the wood on your right.

2 (*For an alternative shorter walk take the left-hand path at the fingerpost past the way-marker and along the green track to the gate. Go through the gate and continue between the farm buildings and through another gate. At the bottom of the track you will cross a very small stone bridge where the tracks make a T junction. Go straight ahead through the gate and cross the field uphill to a stile just to the right of the tree on the horizon. Go over this stile and continue straight ahead across the next field to the next stile, again by a tree. Go over this stile into the road and turn right. At the cross-roads turn left, and continue along this road for about a kilometre to point 6.*) At the fingerpost take the right-hand path past the waymark and go through the gate. Go uphill with a farm below you on your left. Go over a stile into a wood and continue going uphill past a waymark and fingerpost. Take care here as the path is narrow and there is a steep drop to your left. Go across the wooden bridge and over two stiles and into a field. Cross the field and continue to a gate, *but look back at the magnificent view behind.* Go through another field and on reaching another gate turn left into the lane and go downhill.

3 After about 100 metres go over a stile to the right by a gate and into a field. Continue down hill keeping the field boundary on your right. Go toward the brick house in view. Pass the waymark and wood on your right. Look at the view ahead. Go through the gate on the right at the bottom of the field and then cross the field to the gate to the left of the clump of trees at the bottom and go into the road and turn right. Cross the entrance to a field immediately on your right and go over the stile on the right of the road, but facing you. Cross the field going uphill. *Look behind at the view.* Go over the next stile and cross the field and over the stile into the road (at this point you may shorten the walk by turning left to the crossroads and then turning right to 6) and turn right. Go along the road for about 400 metres over the brow and go over the stile on the left.

4 Keep the field boundary on your right and go toward the top of the field. Go through the second gate on your right and turn immediately left and go through another gate. *Admire the view to your right.* Go over the brow and towards the white house keep-

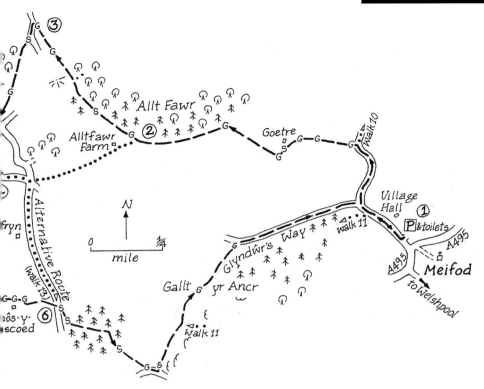

ing the field boundary on your left. At the white house go through the gate and turn right along the farm track. Go through two gates and turn sharp left at the second by the corner of the wood on your left. Go through another gate with the woods on your right until you meet the waymark.

5 At the waymark on the left of the track turn sharp left and backwards diagonally across the field and through the gate. Follow the green track with the wood on your left past the next waymark. Go over a stile and into a field and then over another stile into the wood. Go over another stile, by a gate, and into a field and, keeping the boundary on your right, continue to stile. Once over this stile keep the field boundary on your left and then at the waymark bear right on the track and through two gates with farm houses on your

right. Keep the field boundary on your right and go round to the gate and into the lane. Turn left and follow the lane to the road.

6 Go across the road and over the stile opposite and then across the field and over another stile. Turn left at the waymark and then at the next waymark bear right. Go over the next stile into a field and continue with its boundary on your right. Go through the gate and turn left in the lane. After just a few metres go over the stile by the gate on your left, past the waymark and follow the green track to a gate, with the wood on your right. At the end of the track go through anther gate onto the road and turn right. Follow this road to the end and turn right towards the village. The car park from where you started is about 100 metres further on your left.

WALK 13

ALLT FAWR AND GARTH FÂCH

DESCRIPTION This is a walk mainly along tracks and footpaths of approximately three and a half hours duration. It is suitable for the moderately fit and sure-footed, sensible shoes are a must. Starting from the car-park in Meifod the outward route takes you up the south side of All Fawr woodland and then across fields to Garthfâch. The return route is across fields and then follows the track to the north-west of Gallt yr Ancr (**WALK 7**). The total route is about 6½ miles in length and gives magnificent views.

START The car park, at Meifod. Grid Ref: SJ 153132

DIRECTIONS From Welshpool, take the A490 northwards. After 7 miles, turn left onto the Meifod road (signposted) and follow it to Meifod. In the village turn right at the junction where on your right there is a car park and toilets.

1 After leaving the car park and recycle centre at Meifod turn right and follow the road. Go past the white cottages and then take the second turn on the left through a gate and follow the track with the rear of a house on your left. Go along a tree lined path (this can be muddy) and through a gate. Keep the edge of the field on your left and then go through a gate. Cross the field with the black and white house ('The Goetre') on your right. Go straight across the drive to this house to the waymark and then the stile and wooden bridge. Turn right and go through the gate and diagonally right across the field and uphill towards the wood. Go through the gate in the corner of the field and onto the green path and then along the tree lined path keeping the wood on your right.

2 At the fingerpost take the right-hand path past the waymark and go through the gate. Go uphill with a farm below you on your left. Go over a stile into a wood and continue going uphill past a waymark and then turn left at the fingerpost. Take care here as the path is narrow and there is a steep drop to your left. Go across the wooden

bridge and over two stiles and into a field. *Cross the field and continue to a gate, but look back at the magnificent view behind.* Go through another field and on reaching another gate turn right into the lane.

3 After about 200 metres turn sharp left and go over the stile. Go uphill towards the left of a clump of trees. *Pause to take in the views to your left.* Go over the stile by the trees, pass a waymark and then go over another stile into a field. Skirt this field keeping the boundary on your left to a gate. Go through this gate and then keep the field boundary on your right to another gate. *The view ahead is typical of the area.* After the next gate, cross the field ahead and then go left and downhill at the waymark on a post to another gate by a red brick shed facing Pen-y-bryn Farm. Turn right here and go along the farm lane, though a gate and then turn left into the road.

4 Continue downhill along the road for about 300 metres and then turn right through a gate and onto a track. There is a building with a corrugated roof just below you on your left. Go through two gates which are close together to form a pen, past a waymark, and then through another gate leading to a field. Keep the field boundary on your right to another gate where you bear left downhill and go toward another gate. Continue on to another gate on the right of the field which leads to a track. Go along this track to a disused quarry on your right and through another gate and pass a house on your left. The track is curving to the right and after the next gate it passes a black and white house on your left as it becomes a green track. Go through another gate and follow the track to the road.

5 Turn left onto the road. After about 400 metres turn left onto the lane leading to Garth Fâch (the finger post is opposite the lane). Continue along the lane and pass through the gate leading to the farm sta-

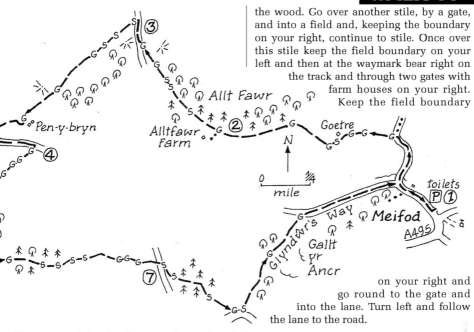

Pen-y-bryn
③
Allt Fawr
Alltfawr
Farm
②
Goetre
④
N

0   ¼
mile

Glyndwr's Way   Meifod
A495
Gallt
yr
Ancr
⑦

toilets
P ①

the wood. Go over another stile, by a gate, and into a field and, keeping the boundary on your right, continue to stile. Once over this stile keep the field boundary on your left and then at the waymark bear right on the track and through two gates with farm houses on your right. Keep the field boundary on your right and go round to the gate and into the lane. Turn left and follow the lane to the road.

bles. Go straight ahead across the yard and through the gate opposite. Bear right and continue downhill toward a stile by the corner of the wood. Go over this stile and across the field and through the gate at the bottom and onto the track. Turn left on the track and pass through two gates close together.

6 At the waymark on the left of the track turn right diagonally across the field and through the gate. Follow the green track with the wood on your left past the next waymark and bear right. Go over a stile and into a field and then over another stile into

7 Go across the road and over the stile opposite and then across the field and over another stile. Turn left at the waymark and then at the next waymark bear right. Go over the next stile into a field and continue with its boundary on your right. Go through the gate and turn left in the lane. After just a few metres go over the stile by the gate on your left, past the waymark and follow the green track to a gate, with the wood on your right. At the end of the track go through anther gate onto the road and turn right. Follow this road to the end and turn right towards the village. The car park from where you started is about 100 metres further on your left.

Meifod

AROUND MEIFOD VILLAGE

DESCRIPTION This walk is a leisurely stroll around the village. Details of many of the buildings are given. Meifod is thought to mean 'temporary lodging'. The earliest church in Meifod was built by St. Gwyddfarch in about AD550. The saint in this case meaning Holy Man. Legends state that when Gwyddfarch was asked where the small church should stand he said: 'yma y mae i fod' — here it is to be. Meifod was the centre of the earliest administration and devotion of St. Tysilio, younger son of the Prince of Powys. In AD1154, Madoc ap Meredydd, Prince of Powys is reputed to have built a church at Meifod and dedicated it to the Virgin Mary. The Norman arches in the vestry and the arch under the tower of the present church are of this period. They are built from red sandstone which was little used in the area and probably expensive to obtain. The main body of the present church was built in AD 1500. In AD 1872 another restoration took place when the west gallery, which was considered unsightly, was removed to expose the handsome pointed arch. The ceiling was also removed to reveal the fine oak roof. Outside in the tranquil churchyard, against the south wall, stood the oldest known gravestone. It is to the memory of the daughter of a William Jones who died 18 May 1670, aged 22 years. The oldest relic inside the church is the crudely carved Celtic stone sited at the west end of the aisle. It was moved here about 150 years ago. It is said to be a vault covering and probably a memorial to a Prince of Powys. The design of the stone is allegorical and the whole is emblematic of the conquest of 'sin'. The first recorded incumbent of the Parish was Madoc ap Llewellyn in 1291. All the registers of the Parish, dating from 1597, are lodged in the National Library of Wales at Aberystwyth. A visit to this ancient seat of Christianity in Wales is well worth the trouble. Here amidst the tranquility of these hallowed grounds one can feel the history of these long begotten times and absorb the feeling of faith and timelessness that these wall and graves embrace.

DIRECTIONS From Welshpool, take the A490 northwards. After 7 miles, turn left onto the Meifod road (signposted) and follow it to Meifod. In the village turn right at the junction where on your right there is a car park and toilets.

1 *Top Shop Tea Shop/The Stores*. Built in 1870 as a police station. Also a laundry. The shop was added in 1921, the Tea Shop in 1999 and a Craft Shop in 2001. Closed in 2005.

2 *'Islwyn'*. A private residence built in the 1930s.

3 *'Maesteg'*. A private residence built in the 1920s.

4 *'Buxton'*. A private residence, formerly a smithy and the smith's sheds can still be seen at the side of the house.

5 *Coach Depot and Garage*. The business developed from a smithy. The former sawpit was reputed to be haunted.

6 *'Lion House'*. Formerly a public house and hotel which closed in 1962.

7 *'Ger-y-nant'*. This house was built over a stream and was the village post office. It has been a butcher's and the slaughterhouse floor still exists in the garden.

8 *'Bank House'*. Formerly the Midland Bank. It closed in the 1990s.

9 *'Vyrnwy House'*. A flat-fronted three-storey residence, noted for its oak door and staircase. It was formerly a hotel with a cellar. Cellars are unusual in Meifod due to the flooding which used to occur. Formerly the village chemist was housed on the ground floor.

10 *'Aldwyn House'*. A private residence that was formerly a saddler, newsagent and a tobacconist.

11 *'Chapel House'*. This is the only remaining house on the old road that used to run parallel with the present road.

12 *Calvanistic Methodist Chapel*. Built in 1874.

13 *Row of houses* which used to be one vast shop where anything could be bought.

14 *'Avalon'*. Formerly a draper's shop.

15 *Elm Villa*. A private residence, but once a busy working area with a blacksmith, carpenter and wheelwright.

16 *'Liverpool House'*. This used to be a shop

noted for its bread. Now a Bric-a-Brac shop.

17 *'Dudley House'*. A private residence, but was the first chapel built by the Weslyan Methodists in 1807.

18 *'Ty Capel'*. As its name implies this was an old chapel.

Gwyddfarch, founded in AD 550. When the foundations were dug buried patterned mediaeval tiles were found.

26 *'Waterloo House'* is early 19th century and presumed to have been built around the time of the Battle of Waterloo. The flat frontage and three bays are typical of the period. The central window is of the 'ogle' type.

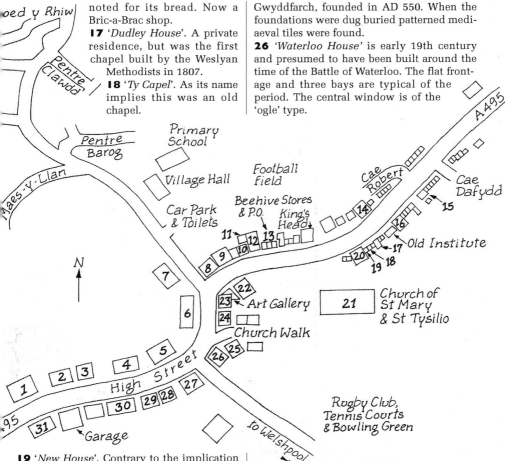

19 *'New House'*. Contrary to the implication of its name, this house is probably the oldest in the village, being 17th century.

20 *'Tŷ Mawr'*. The loft in this house once housed a group of weavers. It was also once a chapel. The blocked up windows were probably a result of the Window Tax.

21 *Church of St Mary & St Tysilio*. The present church is the third dedication. See separate description.

22 *This building* was the Church School up to the Second World War.

23 *Old Post Office*.

24 *'Central House'*. This was formerly the main village shop, built in the 18th century. It was once a farm.

25 *Welsh Independent Chapel*. Build on the site of the original church in Meifod, Eglwys

27 *Calvanistic Methodist Chapel*. Built in 1874. Now two private residences.

28 *'Old Smithy'*. Recently rebuilt.

29 *'Maldwyn'*. Formerly occupied by a tailor who displayed his wares in the bow fronted windows.

30 *Watchmakers*. A block of four small houses, the end one of which housed a watchmaker. Before then it was used as a business to make wooden pumps. These pumps were made by boring lengthways through the trunk of an oak tree. This took about a week of careful labour. The smithy opposite **(4)** made the iron fittings for the pumps.

31 *Bungalow*. A private residence built in 1981.

WALK 15

BRONIARTH HILL

DESCRIPTION This is a 3½ mile walk of approximately two hours duration along lanes, tracks and footpaths. It is suitable for the moderately fit and sure-footed: sensible shoes are a must. Starting from the car-park in Meifod the outward route takes you up the south side of Broniarth Hill. Dominating the skyline to the east of the village is Broniarth Hill. The summit of the hill is about 270 metres above sea level. Although the hill is still wooded much felling has taken place in recent years. Half way along the walk and to the east of Broniarth Hill you will see Llyn Du pool. The return is through the woods, but there are spectacular views of the Vale of Meifod, Allt-y-Main and the River Vyrnwy meandering through the valley.

START The car park, at Meifod. Grid Ref: SJ 153132

DIRECTIONS From Welshpool, take the A490 northwards. After 7 miles, turn left onto the Meifod road (signposted) and follow it to Meifod. In the village turn right at the junction where on your right there is a car park and toilets.

1 Turn left out of Meifod Car Park and proceed the 50 metres to the main road. Turn right and walk about 100 metres then turn left and continue past the bowling-green and tennis courts on the left before crossing the River Vyrnwy by Broniarth Bridge.

2 At the road junction with Ffordd Glyndŵr to the left continue straight ahead up the hill. After about 150 metres fork left through a way marked gate. Continue straight up the field with the field boundary on the right. Just before the far corner of the field there is a waymark on the fence which directs you across the field to a gate at the upper corner. Go through this gate and then proceed steeply uphill to pass the telegraph pole to the way marked post at the top. Behind and to the right of this post go over the stile into the wood.

3 Follow the path uphill through the wood. After a way marked post this path eventually widens out into a track. At the top where there is a way-marked post on the left turn right onto a wider green path near the edge of the forest. Cross the forest track and pass the way-marked posts and follow the path behind a large house and garden on the right. Go over the stile cross the field.

4 Shortly a lake appears on the right. Stop and admire the view. *It is worthwhile stopping here for a short rest and having your refreshments – if you have brought any!* Follow the raised green path which winds around the edge of the woodland on the left. Go over two more stiles and into the field at the top. Here there is a three-way junction. Ignore the track uphill immediately to the left and with the water tank on the left go downhill about 20 metres to a gate marked as 'Glyndŵr's Way' on the left. Go through the gate and along the path through the forest. Pass a way marked post on the left. Eventually you will come to part of the forest which has been cleared giving a magnificent view of Meifod. On entering the forest again continue straight on down the path until you come to a junction with an unmetalled road which bends around here. Continue downhill to the junction with the road which is Ffordd Glyndŵr. After about a quarter of a mile this road will make a junction with the road you had proceeded up earlier. Turn right and retrace your route into Meifod.

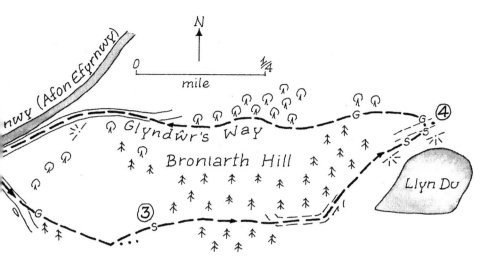

Broniarth Hill

WALK 16
COBHAM'S GARDEN

DESCRIPTION This is a walk along lanes, tracks and footpaths of 3½ miles and approximately two hours duration. It is suitable for the moderately fit and sure-footed, sensible shoes are a must. Starting from the car-park in Meifod the outward route takes you across the River Vyrnwy and through a field known as 'Cobham's Garden' which is hidden away off a lane to the south-east of the village is a small amphitheatre. This is a magical place and was the scene of the capture of John Oldcastle, Lord Cobham, whose religious beliefs differed from those of the 'establishment'. After adroitly escaping from the King's men, he was finally captured in this remote spot. He put up a valiant struggle, but an old woman, who had come along to see the commotion, struck his legs with her milking stool and managed to break at least one of them. Lord Cobham was taken to London where he was hanged on 14th December 1417.
START The car park, at Meifod. Grid Ref: SJ 153132
DIRECTIONS From Welshpool, take the A490 northwards. After 7 miles, turn left onto the Meifod road (signposted) and follow it to Meifod. In the village turn right at the junction where on your right there is a car park and toilets.

1 Turn left out of Meifod Car Park and proceed the 50 metres to the main road. Turn right and walk about 100 metres then turn left onto the Guilsfield road and continue past the bowling green and tennis courts on the left before crossing the River Vyrnwy by Broniarth Bridge.

2 At the road junction where Ffordd Glyndwr diverges to the left keep straight ahead up the hill. Pass a way marked gate, which is Walk No.2 and continue until a way marked gate is seen on the right behind Pen-y-lan Hall. Go through this gate and then over a stile in the corner on the left into the field. Continue uphill over the field to the stile in the top corner and to the right of the roof that is first seen on the skyline. When crossing the field take a pause and turn back to admire the view. Go over the stile and continue uphill and to the right in the lane.

3 After approximately 250 metres go left over the stile by the gate into the field. Go along the short track to the right and then bear slightly left diagonally across the field (note the view to the right). Next go over the stile ahead into the wood and along the narrow way-marked track through the wood until a stile on the left takes one into Cobham's Garden. Immediately, bear right with the hedge on the right, under a tree arch and across a small boggy stream. Shortly a waymark post is reached showing the junction of two walks. Ignore the track to the right and go straight ahead following a green lane. Go through the gate and continue until a gate is sighted ahead at the end of the lane. Take the path to the left and go up through the wood and across the forestry track.

4 Continue uphill with the wood on the right until a stile is reached. Go over the stile and across the field past the finger post which is adjacent to what looks like the remains of a very small quarry working. Walk towards the waymark post in the line of trees ahead. Go through the gap in these trees to the right of the waymark post. Keeping the hedge on the right, continue to a wooden gate at a small farm. Continue through this gate and with a barn on the left go through a second wooden gate. Keep the barns on the left until a third wooden gate is reached on the left at the corner of the barn. Go through this gate and yet another wooden gate and continue ahead through the field and over the brow of the hill to the waymark post on the edge of the forest. Go through the wood by way of the path diagonally to the right and over the stile by the 'Fire' sign. Continue downhill by the very steep forest track. On coming out of the trees pause for a while and admire the views of Meifod to the left. *This is an excellent spot to tarry a while for refreshment (which you will have brought with you?).*

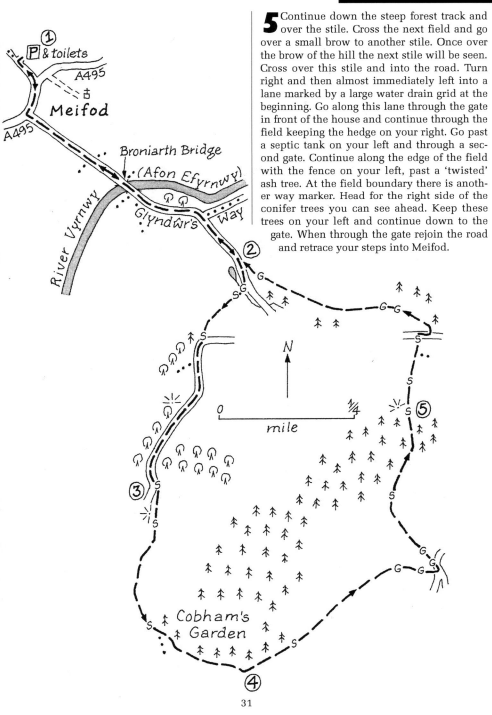

5 Continue down the steep forest track and over the stile. Cross the next field and go over a small brow to another stile. Once over the brow of the hill the next stile will be seen. Cross over this stile and into the road. Turn right and then almost immediately left into a lane marked by a large water drain grid at the beginning. Go along this lane through the gate in front of the house and continue through the field keeping the hedge on your right. Go past a septic tank on your left and through a second gate. Continue along the edge of the field with the fence on your left, past a 'twisted' ash tree. At the field boundary there is another way marker. Head for the right side of the conifer trees you can see ahead. Keep these trees on your left and continue down to the gate. When through the gate rejoin the road and retrace your steps into Meifod.

P & toilets

A495

Meifod

A495

Broniarth Bridge

(Afon Efyrnwy)

Glyndŵr's Way

River Vyrnwy

N

0   ¼
mile

Cobham's Garden

PEN-Y-FOEL

DESCRIPTION The outward walk is along a country lane, and continues up tracks and footpaths through woodland. The walk goes around the hill, Allt Fawr, and then crosses fields on the return to Meifod. It is fairly strenuous and is only suitable for the moderately fit and sure-footed, sensible shoes are a must. Allow about 2 hours for this 4½ mile walk.

START The car park, at Meifod. Grid Ref: SJ 153132

DIRECTIONS From Welshpool, take the A490 northwards. After 7 miles, turn left onto the Meifod road (signposted) and follow it to Meifod. In the village turn right at the junction where on your right there is a car park and toilets.

1 After leaving the car park and recycle centre at Meifod turn right and follow the road. After about one kilometre take a right fork along a narrow road marked as a 'No Through Road'. After about 200 metres turn left over a stile and cross a field to a gate. Cross another field and pass through another gate. Continue through the next field to yet another gate and then continue into the yard. Turn right here and go up the steps facing you, where there is a waymark on the steps. Follow this track with the fence on your left until a gate is reached. Pass through this gate into the road and turn left.

2 Go along this road for about 350 metres and take the road junction on your right by the gate marked 'Gelli Farm'. Continue up this road and over the cattle grid. (*There are pleasant views on your right*). On reaching the 'T' junction of tracks turn left and go through a gate where there are barns on your left, and then turn right and go through another gate. Follow the track steeply uphill to another gate in open ground. Pass through this gate and continue on the track forking left after about 100 metres. The track leads through ferns and past a waymark on a log. On reaching the derelict house of Pen-y-Foel bear right.

3 Go to the right of the derelict buildings following the waymarks and then bear left towards an oak tree. Cross over two stiles and enter the woods. Follow the track steeply downhill. This track twists and turns, but is well marked with fingerposts. When you reach the finger post where there is a track coming in on your right, continue ahead and downhill and fork right passing a waymark before reaching a stile. Continue downhill to the gate after which you will reach another track where there is a finger post.

4 Go ahead onto this track and bear right at the fork. Continue along this tree-lined track until you eventually pass out of the wood, continue on the track amid ferns leading to another gate. After this gate go downhill across the field heading for the gate which is to the right of the derelict building. After passing this gate bear left and go over

the stile before passing the waymark and crossing the drive to the 'Goetre' which can be seen on your left. On the other side of the drive pass the waymark and bear left into the trees. Next bear right through the gate and continue keeping the field boundary on your right. Pass through another gate and along a tree-lined track, passing barns on your right, to another gate through which you go into the road and turn right. Continue along this road into Meifod where you will find the car park on your left from where you started.

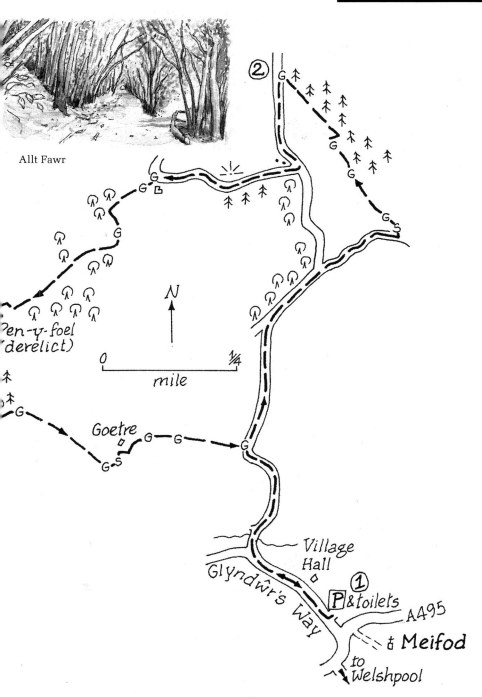

Allt Fawr

②

Pen-y-foel
(derelict)

N

0 ————— ¼
mile

G

Goetre G — G

G-S

Village
Hall

Glyndŵr's Way

①

P &toilets

A495

t Meifod

to
Welshpool

PENIARTH

DESCRIPTION This is a strenuous walk of approximately three hours duration along lanes, tracks and footpaths. It is suitable for the fit and sure-footed, and sensible shoes are a must. Starting from the car-park in Meifod the outward route takes you up Allt y Main (**WALK 10**). It continues downhill through Peniarth Wood and then returns uphill across fields and Glascwm. It is a 6½ mile walk.
START The car park, at Meifod. Grid Ref: SJ 153132
DIRECTIONS From Welshpool, take the A490 northwards. After 7 miles, turn left onto the Meifod road (signposted) and follow it to Meifod. In the village turn right at the junction where on your right there is a car park and toilets.

I After leaving the car park and recycle centre at Meifod turn right and follow the road. After about one kilometre take a right fork along a narrow road marked as a 'No Through Road'. After about 300 metres go through a gate and continue on the forestry track straight ahead. Go through a gate and continue uphill along the forestry track. (*Admire the views on your right*). After about two kilometres from leaving Meifod you will see a footpath to your left which goes up steeply through the forest which is marked as closed because of tree obstructions. Ignore this path and continue around the bend to a waymark on a new footpath on your left.

2 Go uphill along this footpath until you arrive at a 'T' junction of the footpaths with a waymark facing you. Turn right here and go downhill passing another waymark. Just before the forest you will arrive at another footpath 'T' junction. Turn left here and after about 100 metres turn right and follow the footpath down hill through the forest. Pass through the gate and follow the track through the field and pass through the gate

at the bottom, passing the barn on your right. Follow the track to the road and turn right.

3 Take the first right through the gate and over the cattle grid and follow the farm lane to Lower Peniarth Farm. Pass through the farmyard and through the double gate onto a muddy track leading uphill. On reaching the waymark turn right uphill and cross the field, aiming for the gap to the left of the tree on its own. On passing the waymark here bear left and cross the corner of the field to a gate. Go through this gate and turn right and, with the field boundary on your right, go uphill and then turn right through the small gate. Cross the field straight ahead to another gate. (*The view behind should not be missed*). On the other side of the field with the boundary on your left pass through a gate and turn right and pass through another gate. Follow the track to another gate through which you turn right in the lane. Pass through another way-marked gate, pass the cottage and barn on your left and follow the track past another cottage to a further gate. The track leads to a white-painted cottage. Pass through a gate, left of the cottage and through another gate and continue up the tree-lined muddy track to a stile in the corner of a field on your right. Keep the boundary of the next field on you right and go over the next stile. Follow the narrow track uphill through the ferns to a 'T' junction with a wider track and facing the forest. Turn right here. *You may turn left to the viewpoint and forestry seat if you desire, and then retrace your steps.*

4 Follow this track for a few metres to the forestry track and turn left. You are now on the forestry track that you came up earlier. Continue along the track downhill, pass through the two gates and into the lane leading to the narrow road. Go straight ahead here and follow the road, eventually going downhill, into Meifod. The car park where you started will appear on your left in due course.

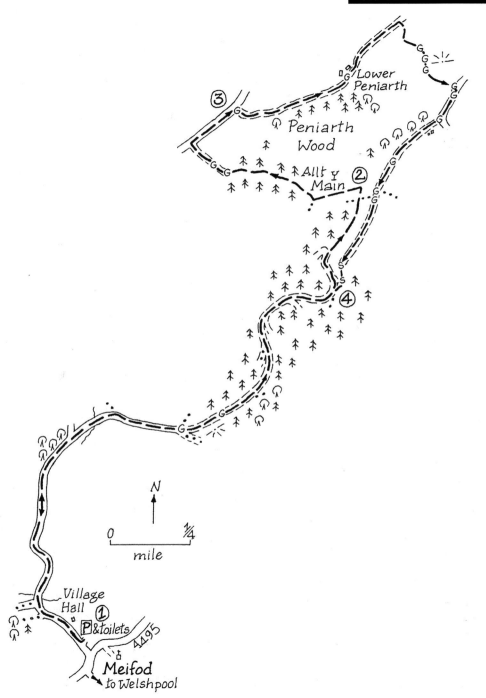

Lower
Peniarth

③

Peniarth
Wood

Allt y
Main ②

④

N

0   ¼
mile

Village
Hall ①
P&toilets
A495

Meifod
to Welshpool

35

BWLCH-Y-CIBAU TO COED-Y-CAPEL

(CIRCULAR)

DESCRIPTION This is an fairly easy walk along lanes, and footpaths across fields of approximately 1½ hours duration. It is suitable for the moderately fit and sure-footed, sensible shoes are a must. The total length of the walk is about 3 miles. Starting from the car-park in Bwlch-y-cibau the outward route takes you to the south of Bwlch-y-cibau. The walk is a figure of eight with one short piece covered twice.

START The car park, at Bwlch-y-cibau. Grid Ref. SJ 178173

DIRECTIONS From Welshpool, take the A490 northwards. After 7 miles, turn right onto the Oswestry road (signposted) and then take the first left towards Llanfyllin. On entering Bwlch-y-cibau the car park is on your right.

1 On leaving the car park and recycle centre at Bwlch-y-cibau turn left and then right along the main road. After a few yards turn left at the crossroads. Take the first right, Ffordd Peniarth or Peniarth Road, and then after about 100 metres turn left down a drive. Pass through the gate by the black shed on your right into the yard and pass the house on your left. Cross the yard and go over the stile facing you. Follow this track and go over the wooden bridge with a stile at the end of it. Follow the tree-lined path with the field boundary on your left, going over a stile, passing through two gates and finally another stile. (Before passing over this stile admire the view behind you). Once over the stile turn left, and follow the track skirting the trees on your right and into a field. Follow the track to the gate but don't go through the gate.

2 Instead, turn about 150 degrees to your right and follow the green track uphill with the trees on your left. *Admire the views behind and to your left.* Follow this track until you almost reach a gate facing you. Just before this gate turn right through another gate.

3 With the field boundary on your right go downhill along the field to another gate. Pass through this gate and bear right and cross the field to a small gate. Go through this gate and turn left (*the view ahead is worth pausing for*). Go down the field with the boundary on your left until, after about 100 metres, you go through the gate on your left. Next make for the gap to the right of the single tree in the row of trees. Go down across the field passing a way-marker on your left and on reaching the way-marker on your right turn right onto the track. Continue along this track passing through a gate until there is a gate in the hedge on your right. Go through this gate and make for the gate at the bottom of the tree-line. On passing through a gate, bear left off the track with the trees on your right and the field fence on your left. Pass the way-marker and go through another gate. Pass another way-marker and go over a stile. You will pass the stile on your left that you came over earlier (you may turn left here and retrace your step back to Bwlch-y-cibau), continue following this track until you reach the gate that you did not pass through earlier.

4 This time pass through the gate into the road and turn left. Follow the narrow road to Bwlch-y-cibau. On reaching the cross roads in the village turn right onto the main-road and then left where you will see the car park entrance.

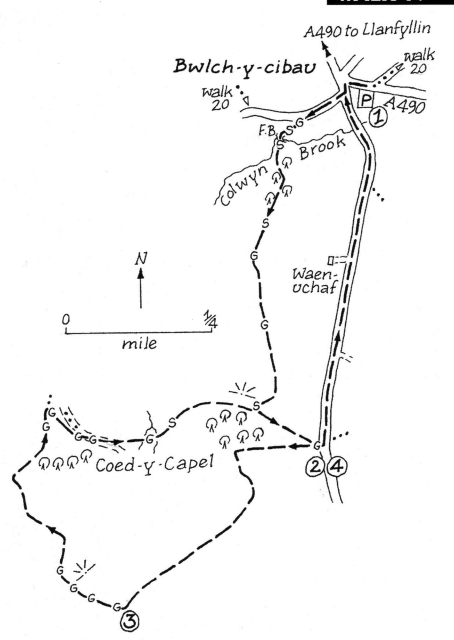

A490 to Llanfyllin

Bwlch-y-cibau

walk 20

walk 20

P A490 ①

F.B. S G

Colwyn Brook

N

0 ¼
mile

Waen-uchaf

G

S

S

G

Coed-y-Capel

② ④

③

BRYNGWYN FROM BWLCH-Y-CIBAU

DESCRIPTION This is an easy walk along lanes, and footpaths across fields of approximately two hours duration. It is suitable for the moderately fit and sure-footed, sensible shoes are a must. The total length of the walk is about 3½ miles. Starting from the car-park in Bwlch-y-cibau the outward route takes you up the south side of Bryngwn Wood. The walk continues through Glan Frogan Woods before emerging onto a road leading to Bwlch-y-cibau. You may return here or turn north and go around Bryngwyn Reservoir.

START The car park, at Bwlch-y-cibau. Grid Ref. SJ 178173

DIRECTIONS From Welshpool, take the A490 northwards. After 7 miles, turn right onto the Oswestry road (signposted) and then take the first left towards Llanfyllin. On entering Bwlch-y-cibau the car park is on your right.

I On leaving the car park and recycle centre at Bwlch-y-cibau turn right and follow the lane. *Excellent views across the countryside can be had almost immediately.* After about one kilometre the lane turns to the right. Leave the lane and turn left onto a track skirting woodland on your left.

2 Continue along this track until it forks. Take the left track and continue gradually to the top of the rise. Ignore the next two tracks going off to the left and continue along the track until it emerges into a lane. Turn left here, and follow this lane, until you reach a fingerpost on the right.

3 (*You may take the shorter walk from here and continue down the lane to the village where you turn left for the car park*).

To continue the full walk, go through the metal gate by the fingerpost, and contour the field keeping the field boundary on your right. Drop down to a way-marked wooden bridge. Go across the bridge and proceed diagonally to a stile by a gate in the far corner of the field and at the top right end of the lake. Go over the stile and continue along the green path which passes to the right of the lake and cross another stile near a gate and by a redwood tree. Go over this stile and straight across the field to another stile near a gate. Once over this stile follow round the curve of the field and slightly to the left to another stile by gates. Go over this stile and head slightly left of the electricity post to a further stile. In the next field, head slightly right to emerge onto a road by a cattle grid. Cross the road and turn left over a stile by a gate and contour the road for a short way. You will cross another stile and then just a few metres further to another stile by a gate which will lead you back onto the road. Turn right and go carefully along the road around the bend to a fingerpost on the right.

4 Turn right into the wood and follow the way-marked path up through the wood. At the top go left and continue along the path to metal gate and steps leading down onto a lane. Turn left here and follow this lane to the village. A left turn and then a right turn bring you back to the car park from where you started

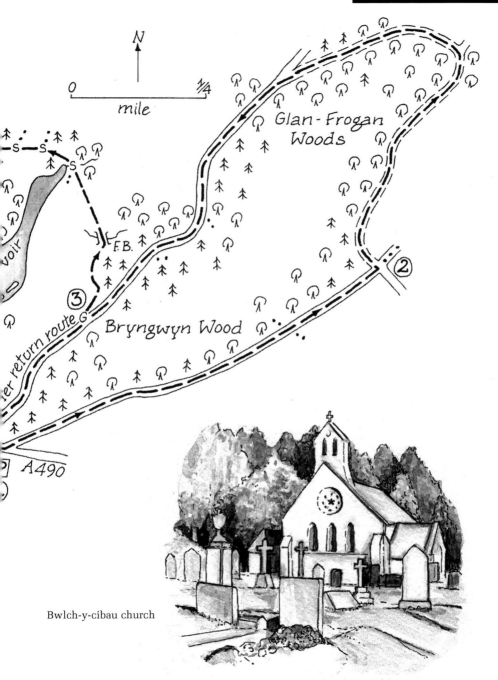

N

0   ¼

mile

Glan-Frogan Woods

S—S S

voir

F.B.

③

er return route

Bryngwyn Wood

②

A490

Bwlch-y-cibau church

PRONUNCIATION

These basic points should help non-Welsh speakers

Welsh	English equivalent
c	always hard, as in **c**at
ch	as on the Scottish word lo**ch**
dd	as th in **th**en
f	as in of
ff	as in o**ff**
g	always hard as in **g**ot
ll	no real equivalent. It is like 'th' in **th**en, but with an 'L' sound added to it, giving '**thlan**' for the pronunciation of the Welsh 'Llan'.

In Welsh the accent usually falls on the last-but-one syllable of a word.

KEY TO THE MAPS

— Main road

═ Minor road

•➤• Walk route and direction

① Walk instruction

– – – Path

∿ River/stream

Ⓖ Gate

Ⓢ Stile

△ Summit

🌲🌳 Woods

▬ Pub

Ⓟ Parking

THE COUNTRYSIDE CODE

• Be safe – plan ahead and follow any signs

• Leave gates and property as you find them

• Protect plants and animals, and take your litter home

• Keep dogs under close control

• Consider other people

The CroW Act 2000, implemented throughout Wales in May 2005, introduced new legal rights of access for walkers to designated open country, predominantly mountain, moor, heath or down, plus all registered common land. This access can be subject to restrictions and closure for land management or safety reasons for up to 28 days a year.

Published by
Kittiwake
3 Glantwymyn Village Workshops, Glantwymyn,
Machynlleth, Montgomeryshire SY20 8LY

© Text & map research: Mike Lister 2008
© Maps & illustrations: Kittiwake 2008
Drawings by Morag Perrott

Cover photos: *Main* – Meifod from Gallt yr Ancr.
Inset – The church of St Tyslio & St Mary, Meifod.
David Perrott

Care has been taken to be accurate.
However neither the author nor the publisher can accept responsibility for any errors which may appear, or their consequences. If you are in any doubt about access, check before you proceed.

Printed by MWL, Pontypool.

ISBN: 978 1902302 61 4